To Terry - Aloha

From Bridget

And

Annie

To Roy, who helped make this dream come true.

Annie Kai Lani Kai Lou

Kauai's Beloved Pup

a sing-a-long book

written, composed and sung by
Bridget Burton

illustrations by
Kathleen Becker

Annie Kai Lani Kai Lou: Kauai's Beloved Pup
Illustrations, Copyright ©2013 by Barbara B. Graf (pseudonym Bridget Burton)
Text, lyrics and musical composition Copyright ©2013 by Barbara B. Graf (pseudonym Bridget Burton)

First Publication 2016
Published by Rockit Press
Gallatin, TN 37066
www.RockitPress.com

Hardcover ISBN 978-0-9962160-5-0
Paperback ISBN 978-0-9962160-6-7
Electronic Book ISBN 978-0-9962160-7-4

Library of Congress Cataloging-in-Publication Data

For information, contact Burton Company Productions, 7644 Girard Avenue, Suite 4, La Jolla, CA 92037.

Printed in the United States of America

www.anniekailani.com

ANNIE KAI LANI KAI LOU: KAUAI'S BELOVED PUP
features the island adventures of Annie Kai Lani
Kai Lou—named in part after the famous Hawaiian
queen and a word often associated with the sea and
the sky. Annie's island activities are as boundless
as her energy—from ziplining, to sailing, golfing,
surfing—even dancing at a luau with a Shih Tzu!
There is a CD that accompanies the book, featuring
Bridget and capturing Hawaiian music in each of
the 10 verses. To purchase the CD or download the
music, visit the website at www.Anniekailani.com.

www.anniekailani.com

*To purchase your
sing-a-long music, go to
www.anniekailani.com
or scan this code.*

Annie Kai Lani Kai Lou

She likes to ride in a canoe
Annie Kai Lani Kai Lou
She goes down the Wailua River
Annie Kai Lani Kai Lou
She's the Hawaiian pup that everyone knew

She's Annie Kai Lani, Annie Kai Lani
Annie Kai Lani Kai Lou
She'll make room in the canoe for you!

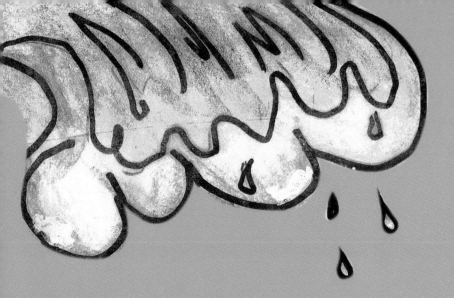

Annie Kai Lani Kai Lou

She likes the beach at Poipu
Annie Kai Lani Kai Lou
She'll surf in the waves with you
Annie Kai Lani Kai Lou
She's the surfer pup that everyone knew

She's Annie Kai Lani, Annie Kai Lani
Annie Kai Lani Kai Lou
Annie Kai Lani loves you!

Annie Kai Lani Kai Lou
She likes the helicopter view
Annie Kai Lani Kai Lou
Says there's a lot in Kauai to do
Annie Kai Lani Kai Lou
She's the flying pup that everyone knew

She's Annie Kai Lani, Annie Kai Lani
Annie Kai Lani Kai Lou
Hopes to fly the helicopter with you!

ANNIE KAI LANI KAI LOU
Plays golf by the ocean blue
Annie Kai Lani Kai Lou
Makes a par on Hole Number Two
Annie Kai Lani Kai Lou
She's the golfer pup that everyone knew

She's Annie Kai Lani, Annie Kai Lani
Annie Kai Lani Kai Lou
Annie Kai Lani loves you!

ANNIE KAI LANI KAI LOU
At the Hyatt working on her Sudoku
Annie Kai Lani Kai Lou
Watching reruns of Jurassic Park II
Annie Kai Lani Kai Lou
The smartest pup that everyone knew

She's Annie Kai Lani, Annie Kai Lani
Annie Kai Lani Kai Lou
Wants your help to finish her Sudoku!

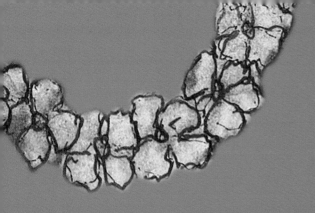

Annie Kai Lani Kai Lou

Says luaus in Kauai are a hoot
Annie Kai Lani Kai Lou
Has fun dancing all night long with a Shih Tzu
Annie Kai Lani Kai Lou
She's the dancing pup that everyone knew

She's Annie Kai Lani, Annie Kai Lani
Annie Kai Lani Kai Lou
Annie Kai Lani loves you!

ANNIE KAI LANI KAI LOU
Sails the Na Pali coast with a crew
Annie Kai Lani Kai Lou
Says the dolphins are spinning on cue
Annie Kai Lani Kai Lou
Thinks dolphins are amazing, don't you?

She's Annie Kai Lani, Annie Kai Lani
Annie Kai Lani Kai Lou
Annie Kai Lani loves you!

ANNIE KAI LANI KAI LOU
Ziplines a hundred feet above you
Annie Kai Lani Kai Lou
Looks like a flying monkey at the zoo
Annie Kai Lani Kai Lou
The zipline pup that everyone knew

She's Annie Kai Lani, Annie Kai Lani
Annie Kai Lani Kai Lou
Says you're gonna be thrilled with the view!

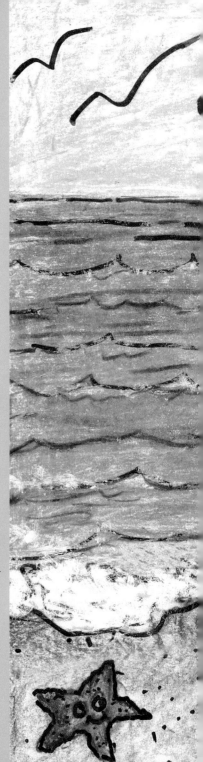

ANNIE KAI LANI KAI LOU
Wags her tail and does the hula too
Annie Kai Lani Kai Lou
Eats Ahi and Opah fish too
Annie Kai Lani Kai Lou
She's the Hawaiian pup that everyone knew

She's Annie Kai Lani, Annie Kai Lani
Annie Kai Lani Kai Lou
Annie Kai Lani loves you!

ANNIE KAI LANI KAI LOU
Needs a rest and wouldn't you too?
Annie Kai Lani Kai Lou
Dreams of when you'll come to visit her soon
Annie Kai Lani Kai Lou
The beloved pup that everyone knew

She's Annie Kai Lani, Annie Kai Lani
Annie Kai Lani Kai Lou
Annie Kai Lani loves you!

ALOHA ʻOE FROM
ANNIE KAI LANI KAI LOU!

Bridget Burton is a published author, business consultant and soft jazz recording artist who decided it was time to write a children's sing-a-long book. She was inspired by the boundless energy and shenanigans of her real English Springer Spaniel Annie and her love of the captivating garden isle of Kauai, Hawaii. Having visited Kauai on vacation, she decided to write about it from the dog's perspective. Bridget lives in La Jolla, California with her husband Roy, their grown children Ryon & Kristina nearby, and, of course, Annie.

Kathleen Becker is an illustrator and artist, who has worked in children's education for more than 20 years. Her understanding of children's inquiring minds and way of learning are combined with her artistic talent in the books she illustrates. Kathleen captures the personalities of the animals she creates in whimsical settings, with just the right mixture of color and design. Kathleen has a grown daughter, Nikki and resides in Los Alamitos, California with her three cats.

Photography: Joanna Herr
Book layout: Shonna Jordan

CPSIA information can be obtained
at www.ICGtesting.com
Printed in the USA
LVIC04n1930041216
515594LV00001B/1

* 9 7 8 0 9 9 6 2 1 6 0 5 0 *